Minimalist Budget Hacks

*Taste the Sweetness of Positive Cash
Flow and Denounce Poverty*

By Phil C. Senior

Table of Contents

Description

This book will help you get your finances in order and finally stop living paycheck-to-paycheck. You will learn how to make your own unique budget, stop hemorrhaging money, how to avoid impulsive splurges, tactics to save more money or start saving money, how you can reduce on your waste, energy usage, and save at the same time, the importance of reconciling your bank statements and how to make a retirement savings plan. After you read this, you'll be able to stick to a budget and save like a pro! So many people have troubles trying to stick to a budget month after month and fail. Many people also have troubles with impulsive spending that causes them to break their budget. What if I tell you that it can actually be beneficial to spend money? Find out how inside!

Introduction

Hello and thank you for downloading *Minimalist Budget Hacks: Taste the Sweetness of Positive Cash Flow and Denounce Poverty* by Phil C. Senior.

Taste the sweetness of positive cash flow!

In this book, you will learn how to make a budget, stop living paycheck-to-paycheck, include a savings plan into your budget, how much you should be saving for retirement, how to stop meaningless spending, how to get yourself to save money instead of spending it, how to create less waste and save money doing so, why you should reconcile your bank account, and how to plan for retirement. We will learn many tactics to save more money, learn that you probably have a lot more wiggle room than you think you do, and we will learn that extra spending in moderation is not only okay but also encouraged! This book will help you make a budget and stick to it. I hope you enjoy the read!

There are a lot of books on this subject, so once again, thank you for choosing this one!

Chapter 1: Basics of Budgeting

A very important lesson when it comes to budgeting is that you should not try to use someone else's budget. Everyone has different needs and you need a unique budget that fits your lifestyle. If you're someone who works from home, you are probably going to require an unlimited internet plan to allow for how much you use your computer. If you use your car for a rideshare app or have a longer commute to work, you need to set a higher monthly allowance for gas and expect to spend more on maintenance since it's being driven more. Create your own unique budget that is going to fit your wants and needs.

The first thing you'll need to do when creating a budget is to write down how much money you're making every month, and how much money you are spending every month.

- Create a list of your total monthly income
    - Any kind of income you consistently get every month will be included in your total monthly income. It can include your wages from your job(s), child support, rental income, etc. Any money that you can rely on to consistently come in every week, bi-weekly, or monthly can be included in this.

- Create a list of necessary monthly expenses
    - Anything that must be paid every month such as rent, electricity, gas, water, trash, groceries, loans, credit card debt, transportation expenses, savings, and medical expenses.

- By breaking all the categories up, it can help you get a better idea of how much you're spending in each area.
  - Housing
    - This would include your rent or mortgage, POA dues, renters or homeowner's insurance.
  - Utilities
    - Includes water, gas, electricity, and trash pickup.
  - Transportation
    - Car payment, car insurance, gas, and maintenance.
  - Household
    - Includes groceries and toiletries.
  - Childcare
    - Babysitters, nannies, daycare, or after school care are included in this.
  - Medical
    - This includes health, life, dental and vision insurance. Along with any prescriptions and copays.

- Debt
    - Student loans, personal loans, and credit card debt.
- Savings
    - Emergency fund and retirement fund.
- Wardrobe
    - Uniforms or any professional work attire required.

- Create a list of all extra expenses you have regularly
    - Includes things like your cell phone, home phone, internet, cable, going out to eat, morning coffee, entertainment, new shoes, clothes, vacation funds, and so on. It's important to include this type of spending in your budget because these are the type of things that people will splurge on, even if they don't have the money for it. By including a little bit of this in your budget, it can avoid feeling like you've restricted yourself too much, and give you some room to enjoy yourself while not overspending.

You'll need to figure out how much of your paycheck you can actually use for spending. Take your after-tax income, and calculate how much you have left after Medicare, Social Security, health insurance, life insurance, retirement contributions, and any other deductions have been taken out. That is the amount you'll have to spend and put towards bills. Once you've written down your fixed income you have coming in each month, then you can begin to calculate all the money you have going out each month. I suggest making a list (as shown above), in order of importance so that when you get to bills that aren't as important or aren't as fixed, you will have some wiggle room if you are starting to get low on your money coming in. For example, your rent/mortgage versus your phone bill. Rent/mortgage is a fixed expense that cannot be negotiated or brought down. The price of a phone bill can be brought down by changing companies, lowering your data plan, or finding discounts. This is a great way to find a little extra room in your budget for more money to put into savings or for some extra spending money.

If you have problems with splurging, it's very beneficial to plan for any extra money you might be spending. If you go out to eat for breakfast every Sunday, like to go out on the weekends, or just want to have a little bit of shopping money, then you should include that in your budget. This is of course if you have a little bit of money left over once you've made a budget for yourself. This is mostly aimed at anyone who has some money to spend but tends to splurge and break their budget when they really want something and end up overspending. Planning for some spending money can avoid impulsive overspending because it doesn't restrict you from doing the things you want to do. It allows for some spending, just not as much as you might spend if it's a spur of the moment decision.

A tactic you can use to distribute your money properly is to use the 50/30/20 rule. This means that 50% of your income will go to needs (housing, utilities, groceries, insurance), 30% will go to your wants (shopping, entertainment, going out to eat, hobbies), and the last 20% will go into savings. To do this, you need to calculate your after-tax income. This is what's left of your paycheck after local, state, and income taxes have been taken out. After these have been taken out, what you have left is your actual income. If you're self-employed, you'll have to take out your own taxes. After you have calculated how much you make after taxes, this is the amount you'll use when figuring the percentages for the 50/30/20 rule. So, if you make $2,000 monthly after taxes, $1,000 should be spent on needs, $600 should be spent on wants, and $400 should be put into savings or used for debt repayments.

So, I've told you the numbers and the importance of sticking to a budget. But why would a budget be beneficial to you? How can a budget help your life?

- Helps you organize your spending and saving

    o Saving is very important and there are multiple different kinds of saving. It would be wise to have an emergency fund and 3-6 months of living expenses. We never expect for things in life to go wrong, but that's also how things can end up even worse. When unexpected things happen, it's a huge relief to at least have your finances taken care of. If you lose your job, your car stops working, or a pipe bursts, you are going to be extremely thankful that you had emergency money. Another type of savings would be your retirement savings plan. This is one of the most important accounts you will have because your last 20-30 years of life depends on you putting enough money in this plan to live off of. This is what is going to replace your income when you retire. It's hard for younger people to grasp the concept of retiring when they are so far away from it. You may just be starting your first real, adult job and can barely deal with trying to figure out what you want to do with the rest of your life. Let alone try to think about what you want to do in retirement. Although it seems so unreachable and far away, we are all going to get there one day. You may not know exactly what your plans are, but it's important to start saving as early as possible. It's never too late to start saving, but it will greatly increase the amount of money you have when you retire the earlier you start.

- Security
  - Having a budget can make you feel secure because you never have to stress about whether or not your bills are going to get paid. You can even make everything automatic and then you really won't have to worry about it! Have a certain amount of money go straight into your savings every time you get paid, and then all the money that you will spend on bills you can keep in your checking account. Set up all of your bills to automatically come out, and then take out cash for any person spending money. This way, you don't ever even see the money that's going away. But you know all of this is working in the background without you having to lift a finger. Without doing anything at all, your bills are being paid, you have money going into savings, and the only money that you see is the money that you're allowed to spend!

- Keeps you out of debt

    o When you don't have a budget, it can be really
      easy to fall into impulsive buying and
      overspending. You get used to being stressed
      about bills and living paycheck-to-paycheck
      because that's what is normal to you. You
      might really want to start a budget every single
      month, but you never take the jump, and
      actually make one and stick to it. It can be
      very hard to get out of the habit of not having
      a budget, but when you finally do start
      working with a budget, that's what will feel
      normal to you and that becomes your habit.
      Not to mention, it's far less stress on you.

- Gives you control over your money

    o Instead of being impulsive and letting your
      money control you, you control the money.
      You decide where it goes and what you are
      going to do with it. You will feel really in
      control when you see your savings start to
      grow!

- Allows you to communicate with your significant
  other

    o One of the biggest reasons couples get into
      fights is about money. It causes unnecessary
      stress and can really put a strain on your
      relationship. When you feel like you aren't
      where you want to be financially, it can be
      embarrassing to talk about your finances, even
      with your significant other. This can really
      drive a wedge between you, because money is

something that involves both of you, and not knowing what is going on financially can make you both feel uncertain. When you start to make a budget and stick to it, you'll become more confident in yourself and in your spending, and will feel much better talking about finances. When you both stick to a budget, this promotes teamwork and keeps you both motivated to do better. If you have other family members or children that live with you, sticking to your budget can teach them how to be responsible and accountable with money.

- Gives you plenty of warning

  o When you plan for the future and look at the "big picture", you'll see money problems coming your way before they even happen, and have time to prepare before they affect you.

- Taking on more debt

  o If you have a budget, then you know exactly how much money you're spending, and exactly how much money you have left every month. Debt isn't a bad thing if you can afford it. It's only when you take on too much debt, or you aren't responsible with your money while you're in debt, is when it causes problems. An auto loan is debt, or if you are thinking about buying a house, your mortgage would be debt. Used correctly, debt can actually be a good thing. Not only does it allow you to get a new car or house, if you make your payments every month on time, then it can improve your credit score too. How you treat your debt determines if it will help or harm you.

- Extra money!

    o Budgeting will allow you to easily find any area where you could be earning more money or spending less.

- Who should make a budget?

    o Well, everyone should make a budget. Both those who might especially need one are people who are working on a limited money, trying to pay off debt, anyone working towards a financial goal, plan on retiring early, and anyone trying to make the most out of their income.

The most important part of a budget is to stick to it. Sometimes making the budget is the easiest part, but carrying it out can be hard. It's very important to prioritize your bills and your spending. You may really want a new outfit, but putting that money in savings is more important. A rule that I have found very helpful is to never spend money that you didn't plan on spending. If it's not in the budget, you do not buy it. Most of the things that we want to buy can be because we're being impulsive. Do not buy it at the moment of wanting it. If you get home and it's still something you want, then you can see if there is room in your budget for a little bit of spending. Go easy on groceries, use water and lights only when needed, anything that will leave you with a little bit of money at the end of the month. If you were successful in finding money in your budget, then you can reward yourself with what you wanted to buy.

Chapter 2: Check Your Bleeding, Especially Subscriptions

Bleeding or hemorrhaging money is when you are spending money on things that you do not need to be spending money on. If you don't pay attention to your expenses, you may not even realize how much money you are putting out to these types of expenditures. This can be getting yourself into debt with loans or credit cards, subscriptions, getting an overdraft or late fees, or anything that you can categorize as unnecessary spending. All of these are things that you can avoid spending money on or don't need. If you are already in debt, then you can't make the debt go away, but you can prevent yourself from getting deeper into debt. Stop using your credit card or anything else that will dig you deeper into the hole that you are in. Instead, budget your money, stop the extra spending and use that money to pay off your current debt and/or loans.

The most common source of bleeding money would be on subscriptions. Individual subscriptions may not seem like you are putting out that much money, but multiple of them can add up quickly. $10 here, another $15 there, it doesn't seem like very much. The issue with subscriptions is that they are banking on people thinking short-term. When presented with the option of spending an upfront cost of $200 yearly, or $20 monthly, most people would opt for the option that is cheaper for them right now. Even if long-term, it's more expensive. That's because most people don't want to spend that amount of money or may not even have that much. But almost everyone has $20 to spend, and that allows you to get the subscription right now. When you think about how much money you're spending every year, then that can show you how out of hand subscriptions can get without you knowing it. A good way to put this into perspective would be to use the rule of 25. This is a way to estimate how much money you'll need for retirement. So, if you're spending "z" amount of money per year, z x 25 = how much you'll need to save for retirement for that specific expense. Let's say that you have 5 subscriptions. 2 of them are $15 a month, 2 are $10 a month, and you have one $50 subscription. That means every month you are spending $100 on subscriptions, and $1,200 yearly. Let's say that you keep these subscriptions all the way into retirement. Going by the rule of 25, $1,200 x 25 = $30,000. That means, $30,000 of your retirement money will be used for your subscriptions every single month. There are so many subscriptions that exist anywhere. You can have food, clothes, and shoes, really anything that you want to be delivered to your doorstep. You don't even have to leave your house for something that you want. If you want a book, you don't have to go to the library, you can just subscribe to an eBook service. If you want clothes, you don't even have to go shopping. You can get a whole new wardrobe delivered to your doorstep! As convenient as subscriptions are, the total price of all of them can creep up out of you and shock when you find out how much you're spending. And sometimes, we may not even know we have a subscription. Something may have renewed without your knowledge, or you were doing a trial that you forget to cancel and now you're paying monthly for it.

A great way to stop bleeding money is to track all your daily expenses. Write down everything that you buy, or you can use a money spending app that tracks your spending. It's easy to get lost in daily spending because a couple of dollars doesn't seem like a lot at the time, but if you do this every single day, then it will add up. Tracking what you spend will help you get a better idea of where your money is going. This will also help you when making your budget and will probably be the first place you should make cuts. For example, if you stop for coffee every day, then you should start making your own at home. If you spend $3 on coffee every day before work, that's $90 you're spending monthly. After the initial cost of a coffeemaker, you can buy coffee and coffee filters that will last you well over a month for less than $20. That change alone would give you an extra $70 every month. Changing small things like this in your daily routine, can free up tons of money that you didn't even realize you were spending so much on. One of the biggest ways people waste money is by eating out. You would not believe how much money this costs you. The problem with eating out or grabbing fast food on your way to, or from work, is that it becomes a habit. Your body starts to get hungry around those times, and you think to yourself that I'll just stop somewhere on the way home, and then I won't have to cook dinner. Or this is the last day I stop and get breakfast on my way to work. But no matter how many times you tell yourself that you're only going to do it for one more day, it ends up happening again. Fast food seems cheap enough. You can't possibly be spending that much money. If you didn't eat this, you would just end up spending the money on groceries anyway, right? And this way you don't have to cook. Wrong. Even though your fast food meal may only cost a couple of dollars, over time it can cost you double, or even triple what you would spend at the grocery store. To give you a real-life example, I'll do the math on picking up fast food 3 times a week, and going out to eat at a restaurant once a week, compared to a budgeted grocery list. Let's say that you pick up fast food 3 times a week at $5 per meal. The restaurant trip cost you $50 assuming you went with a date or a friend. So, $5 x 3 = $15. $15 + $50 = $65. You spend an extra $65 on 4 meals every week. That's not even including the other meals you will have to buy since 4 meals is not going to last you the whole week, some grocery shopping will still be required. Let's say the rest of your groceries cost you $50. So, $50 for groceries and $65 to go out to eat equals $115. There are plenty of meal prep recipes online that cost $50 or less every week. That means, your entire grocery budget is less than what you would spend on 4 meals. Weekly you would spend $65 less, and monthly you would save $260! Just think about what else you could do with that money. Make meals at home and you can cut out a huge chunk of what you're spending on food. To give one more example because you may not go out to eat at a nice restaurant, and let's say you only eat at fast food restaurants that are really cheap. Eating a $5 meal, twice a day will equal to $10 daily. That doesn't sound too bad, right? Well, weekly that would be $70 and monthly that would come to $280. Compared to the $50 grocery budget that would come to $200 at the end of the month. Even eating really cheap and only twice a day, still costs $80 more than going to the grocery store, and getting food that you can eat more of and more frequently. Now, do you see the importance of sticking to a budget? It might seem like it wouldn't save you very much money, but when you consider how much you're spending weekly, monthly, or even yearly, your impulsive extra spending can cost you a substantial amount.

Chapter 3: Trust Yourself Over Advertisements

Understanding when to trust your instincts is an important piece of becoming stronger financially. Learning how to build and maintain a budget will naturally strengthen your confidence, and shape who you are as a responsible consumer and cunning investor. There are many advertisements out there promising lower rates, higher profits, less investment, more time, and an easy answer. As you build yourself up, both financially and personally, you will find that there are no easy, quick answers. Real success is incremental and comes from routine and practice. You will realize that advertisers have one goal in mind — they want to increase their own wealth. Their game plan is in direct opposition to yours.

Increasing one's own wealth is a goal that everyone shares, but there is only a finite amount of wealth to go around. Corporations design advertisements with empty promises to portray the illusion of fighting on the same side as you. As you are building your financial independence, they want to be there to appear to be building with and beside you. They want to seem like they are using their vast resources and power to help the little guy. The truth is that no one got to the top thinking entirely selflessly. No one is going to hand out the secrets to financial success, for any price tag. Those kinds of strategies are more valuable than any price that could be placed on them. A fisherman does not share his secret spot with every fisherman on the lake. Coaches do not sell their secret plays to their opponent. You should not trust an advertisement that promises a backdoor way to the top.

As you learn how to build a budget, you find that the only true way to financial success is managing your own resources.

As you go about discovering what your comfort levels of saving and spending are, you will develop tactics to live well within those levels. You will develop stronger instincts in this new territory, as you learn what the rules of the games are. What once looked like a promising advertisement will become blatantly obvious as to what their actual goal is.

The most rewarding aspect of saving and budgeting is when you find your own path, and most importantly, your own confidence. Maintaining a budget is comparable to working out and eating right. It takes practice. It takes a routine that you rigidly hold yourself to. You must learn how to deny yourself immediate gratification in order to become much happier later. A good way to go about this is to pay attention to how you feel when you need resources and do not have them, and how you feel when you have resources and do not need them. Compare the feelings. Do you feel a slight guilt when you splurge when you really shouldn't? Do you feel regret when your tire blows out and the bottom of your wallet is painfully visible? When you save, you are rewarding yourself. You are not buying that splurge item now, but you are buying peace of mind later. You are buying a consistent, smooth ride through your day, week, or month. The more you save, the stronger your "rainy day" allowance becomes, and as you practice your routine and self-control, the stronger your confidence will become. Being the savior of your own day will be more rewarding than that detour through the drive-through.

As your routine becomes more, well, routine, you will find that your comfort level is not set in stone. Your level of comfortable living will mold to what your resources will allow. This is not to say that you must live in squalor to survive, but it should be mentioned that your lifestyle will change as you allocate more of your energy and effort into your financial success. This goes back to advertisements. Your belongings are not inferior because the next generation of products is on television. You will not be judged because your phone, or car, or clothes are not the latest model. Another tactic for a successful advertisement is to create not a want, but a need for their product. They want you to believe that you must throw away all of your belongings, and buy all new products immediately. They will make you believe that it is easier to buy a new product than to live with or fix your own. Some will argue that buying a new product saves you time over repairing your own, and that time equals money. Well, how much money did you spend on your beloved belongings, and how much will you spend on the new model? Does your current item even need to be repaired? Is it possible or even comfortable to go on living with what you have? Would you have had that need for the new product if you had not seen that advertisement?

The real challenge is believing that there is happiness in saving. Advertisements will promise happiness now, and initially, it does not seem that self-denial is any fun. Advertisements are designed to be infectious and remain everywhere, all of the time. It is difficult to avoid the siren's song of a new phone, especially when your other option is to not buy that phone. The kicker is that those who know the everlasting happiness of planning for your future are those who have done it, and those who have lived in immediate gratification will be skeptical of any more satisfying lifestyle, especially when it is reinforced by the constant barrage of advertisements. Unfortunately, the most common way for those to learn how to plan for failure is to experience failure, and not just once. Some people need repeating and harsh life lessons to learn how to prevent relearning the same lesson. The bright side to this is, much like any positive routine you could have in your life, is that once you see the rewards of it once, it is hard to go back to how you used to live and spend. You will experience a sense of pride and enjoyment that is new and different from the same splurges that you have become used to. It will be a reward that is guilt free, even. You will want to continue to experience this. It will become easy to think ahead and remain aware. It will become more rewarding than anything that you have experienced financially. You will happily skip the next immediate impulse and find that it is not self-denial, but self-gratification.

The bottom line for this portion is awareness. Awareness as a consumer, and awareness as a person. Trusting an advertisement over your own instincts is a lack of confidence in your own practices and a lack of awareness for what the actual objective of that corporation's advertisement is. Being aware of who you are and how you feel in every moment, allows you to make sensible decisions to either further experience those feelings, or avoid those feelings. As you build your budget and practice your routines, you will find your center. You will find your comfort level, and you will discover that your comfort level will change as you have more or fewer resources available to you. You will become a person who does not define their needs by what is being advertised, but a person who forges their own lifestyle based on personal needs, and a growing confidence in what they can achieve through their own practices. Building a budget and living inside of it will define you as a person more than the call of an advertisement ever will. You will discover who you are and will be happier for it. Buy yourself your own comfort.

Chapter 4: Save Before Spending

There are a lot of things that we save for. Short-term saving can include things like vacations, emergency funds, anywhere from a few months to a years' worth of living expenses, down payment for a car, etc. Long-term saving can include a down payment for a house, saving for your child's education, retirement, etc. If you're saving long-term, then you are probably using some sort of savings account. You can set it up so that the money automatically goes into the account without you ever having to touch it. If you're saving short-term, here are a few tactics to being able to save money even on a tight budget and keep yourself on track.

- Daily savings

  o Simple fixes to your daily routine can save you quite a bit of money. Saving just a few dollars a day by avoiding impulse buying something that you don't need, or making something cheaper can add up, and by the end of the month, you'll have some extra money that you can use to put into savings. You can do this by using coupons when you go grocery shopping, watching a movie at home instead of in the theaters, dine out less, and cook at home more often. There are many changes you can make that will give you some extra money at the end of the month.

- Use different apps and tools to help you save

  o There are tons of apps today that will help you save money. They track your spending and do all the work for you. Some of them will automatically transfer your money into a separate account when you want it transferred. Others will track your spending and every time you make a purchase will round up to the nearest dollar amount and put the money in a separate savings account. This is really useful because it's a very small amount of money that's taken out so that you won't notice the money being gone, but if you are a frequent spender then it can add up quickly.

- Save your change
  - Like the app we just talked about, saving your change isn't very much money to put back, but you would be surprised by how much money you can accumulate by saving all the coins that you come into contact with. This could be money that you save every week, you can use it for gas money, extra spending money, or put it towards a bill or your weekly grocery budget.

- Groceries
  - Make a grocery budget. It's very easy to overspend on groceries if you aren't careful. This is an area that you can go way over on your budget every month or cut down on spending a lot and even have money left over. Meal prep, which is a topic we will talk more about, is a great way to reduce your grocery budget because you plan for what you're going to buy, and you buy in bulk which cost

less when you consider the amount of food you are getting.

- Monthly bills

    o Most of your bills are a fixed expense that can't be lowered, but there are a few that you may be able to save on. Check to see if you qualify for any discounts with your phone or cable bill. If you are not using all that is included in your plan, downgrade to a lower and cheaper plan, or entirely switch your plan if there is a cheaper option. You could also see if it would be cheaper to bundle your cable and internet. Save on your electric bill by turning off any lights when you aren't in the room, and turn off the T.V if no one is watching. Take shorter showers and don't leave the sink running when you do the dishes. Instead, fill up one side of the sink with hot water to clean your dishes. This can help to lower your water bill. You may also be able to lower your car payment by refinancing your auto loan and getting a lower interest rate.

Everything above could also be used to increase your long-term savings. Anywhere you make room could be more money that you put back into an emergency fund, vacation fund, your retirement, or an education fund.

A great way to save money is to pay yourself first. This is a tactic in which you put money away for savings before you pay any bills. By doing this, it's getting rid of any extra money you may have spent, and putting it towards your savings instead. Doing this will get you out of the mindset that you have extra money to spend, and keep you on track with your budget. Saving will take some time for you to reach your goals. The only way to progress is slowly and consistently. When you do reach your goals, and even in the process of reaching them, here are a few examples of the benefits you'll get from paying yourself first.

- You'll feel a sense of security

  - It's comforting to know that your bills are paid for and that you have some savings put away. It gives you a feeling of security knowing that if something bad happens, you have an emergency fund to take care of it. When you see the numbers in your account growing, you'll feel proud and a sense of accomplishment. You'll feel good about yourself knowing that you are in control of what's in your bank account, and as that number continues to grow, you'll only feel better. In time, it will feel more and more natural to pay yourself as you form a habit of doing it every time you get paid.

- You'll have investment capital

  - In order to make investments, you'll need capital. If you ever want to get into real estate or start your own business, you will need capital to do this, and you'll be able to use the money that you've been saving to do so. You should never use the money you put aside for anything other than investments that will appreciate in value.

- Money for retirement

o Most retirement plans are pre-taxed, which means any contributions made to these accounts are not taxed. Accounts that are pre-taxed include 401(k), 403(b), and IRA accounts. They will only be taxed when you retire, but you can enjoy the accounts being tax-free until then along with the interest you are acquiring.

- Reaching your goals

    o You don't have to start out with impossible goals to reach and an airtight budget. It's really better if you don't. We all want to reach our goals and keep progressing, but setting expectations too high is only setting yourself up for failure. Start with baby steps and work your way up to harder goals to reach. If you are still living paycheck-to-paycheck, start with making an easy to follow, simple budget. You don't even need to include savings at first. Just start out by setting aside all the money that is going to be taken out for bills each month. Then work your way up to making a grocery budget, then work out a way to include savings, then you can start towards having an emergency fund and retirement plan, along with a few months of bills saved. Then you can keep working from there to whatever goals you want to accomplish. The biggest goal will be learning how to adapt to living on a budget, instead of spending money when you feel like it, then being broke at the end of the month. Breaking this cycle will be your biggest first step. You may have to sacrifice a few things in the beginning when you're getting used to your budget. It will soon become a habit and will be worth it when you see the money start to pile up.

Chapter 5: Zero Waste

There are many ways to reduce your waste. Not only is it good for the environment, but it'll be great for your wallet too.

- Food
  - o Food not being used or eaten and going bad is a really big problem if you're trying to cut down on waste and cut down on your grocery bill.

- Paper products
  - o Almost all paper products and other disposables can be replaced with a reusable option. These options are usually a little bit higher in price initially, but since you don't throw them away, you can keep using them instead of buying more, which will ultimately save you money and cut down on wasting a lot of product.

- Clothes
  - o Buying used clothes does not mean having to wear someone's raggedy hand-me-downs. There are many apps now that allow people to sell or trade their old clothes that have been kept in good condition. For a great discount too! You could even sell some of your old clothes you don't wear anymore for some extra spending money.

- DIY household products

- There are plenty of websites that show tutorials on how to make your own household products. This can range from food items to cleaners to makeup. There are TONS of DIY recipes for household products on the internet. By making your own products, you know exactly what is in each one, and you don't have to worry about any harsh chemicals that may be in any of them. This is also a great way to reduce waste, and the cost to make your own products is far less than buying them.

- Consuming less

  - Consuming less means you're creating less waste. Which in turn means saving time and money. When you consume less, it will more than likely make you conscious of the items that you are buying and what is inside them. This will eventually lead you to be more careful about the price of the items you buy, as well as reducing any impulsive spending since you are paying attention to what you're buying.

Along with trying to create less waste, a way to cut some of your spending is by making a grocery budget. Groceries are really easy to go over on because most people don't make a plan for the grocery store. You go in and grab the food that you want, or whatever looks good and accept whatever price you must pay. You should have a grocery list that fits your grocery budget before you ever even step foot in the store. A great way to do this is by meal prepping. You will have a list of foods that you plan to buy, and that is the only thing you should buy while you're there. There are tons of meals prepping recipes online that are healthy and budget-friendly, so there is no reason you should have to add anything else to your grocery list. There are even meal prep recipes that cost as low as $1 per meal for the whole week! Pick a recipe that you think you would enjoy that fits your budget and stick to only that. Since you know what food you're getting ahead of time, you should be able to have a pretty good guess about what you'll be spending, so you know that you'll be within your budget even before you go shopping. You can make meals for your whole week and this will greatly reduce your food waste. Since you make all your food for the week in one day, you'll have tons of extra time throughout the week because your cooking is already done. And time is money!

When you try to find meal prepping recipes online, most of the pages that come up are "how to meal prep on a budget". Meal prepping was meant to be inside your grocery budget. It's all about planning. It can be a great way to fit into your grocery budget while helping you reach your health goals too. A study was done that shows that people who spend more time preparing what they're going to eat, are more likely to make better choices. The more you think about what you're going to eat, the less likely you are to eat impulsively. Which sounds very similar to sticking to a budget! The more you pay attention to the money you are spending, the less likely you are to spend impulsively. That same study done also shows that spending more time preparing your food, means you're less likely to go out to eat and choose fast food. You might think that healthy eating is reserved for people who have a lot of money to spend on groceries, and tons of time to cook it. It's actually the complete opposite. Meal prepping is known to be very cheap and cuts out a ton of time that you would spend cooking throughout the week. It saves you time and money, as well as making you healthier. Here's how to make a meal prepping plan.

- Make a plan

  o You should decide on a recipe in your price range that will fit your grocery budget. Make a grocery list so you'll know exactly what you'll be getting at the store before you go. This will prevent spending money on things you don't need. Stick to your plan!

- Shop in bulk

  o You'll be making food for days or a week. Buy in bulk so you can make your weeks' worth of groceries and get a discount for buying more. Not only does buying in bulk save you money, but you also avoid spending extra money on name brand food.

- Shop seasonally

  o Your local farmer's market can be a fresher and possibly even a cheaper choice.

- Get your quantities right

  o Buying in bulk may save money, but if the food you're buying isn't stored properly or isn't used, you can end up wasting a lot more food than you normally would have. If you are freezing any food, you should write the date on it so you know how long it has been in there. Then you'll know if you can still use it or if it needs to be tossed.

- Get cooking!

  o Set a few hours aside one day of the week, and start cooking all the food you'll be eating over the next week. Once the food is cooked, make sure you divvy out the food in correct portion sizes.

A great way to save money and reduce waste is to save energy! By reducing your electric and water usage, you are not only saving money, but it's also great for the environment. There are many ways you can save energy and reduce the amount of water you're using. I will list a few ways you can do so.

- Wash clothes on cold

  o Using cold water requires less energy.

- Use dryer balls in the dryer

- o These balls are inexpensive and cut down on drying time.

- Replace light bulbs

  - o When your bulbs burn out, you should replace them with LED light bulbs. You can buy a pack of 6 for $12.99 online, and they are estimated to last for 13.7 years, and they are much more efficient than other bulb options.

- Thermostat

  - o Changing your thermostat just a couple of degrees can save you hundreds every year!

- Do some of your chores at night

  - o Utility companies will actually charge you more for using energy during peak hours of the day. Avoid this by running the dishwasher and/or the washing machine at night when energy costs are lower. Not all companies go by this rule, and it will only affect the cost if your utility company uses dual time. If they use a flat rate, then it doesn't matter what time you use it.

- Air dry your clothes

  - o During colder months, you may not be able to do this, or you might be able to hang up your clothes somewhere inside. But if you do hang them outside, your clothes will smell amazing! Most people really enjoy the smell of laundry hung out to dry outside.

- Unplug

- o Unplug anything that you aren't using. Even if it's turned off, it can still use up energy by being plugged in. So, if you really want to save, get in the habit of unplugging things when you're done using them. It might be easier to plug everything into a power strip and unplug the whole strip when you aren't using it.

- Check for discounts
  - o Contact your utility company and see if they have any discounts available, or if you qualify for any savings programs. Don't be shy to call and ask! The worst thing they can say is no and you might end up saving some money.

- Avoid the draft
  - o Here are a few things that you can do to avoid a draft. Make sure windows are sealed, install weather stripping around doors, and you can install insulation pads inside of your outlets. These will all decrease your utility costs by reducing the cold air that's let inside your house.

- Fans
  - o Use ceiling fans or floor fans when possible instead of turning on the AC.

- Shower heads and faucets
  - o You can purchase shower heads and faucets that are more energy and cost efficient but will require some money up front. Your

savings will eventually cover the cost of the items.

- Install a programmable thermostat

  o You can set the temperature to be lower when you're at sleep or not home. This avoids heating or cooling an empty house which is a complete waste of money and energy. There are even some utility companies that will install the thermostat for you. The only difference you'll notice is that your bill is lower.

All of these are very helpful ways to reduce the energy you're using and to lower your utility costs. Whether you want to help the environment, lower your bill, or both, any of these options can be useful to you.

Another great way to save energy and money is to get outside! If it's a nice day, you can spend the day outside instead of being inside using energy all day. If you aren't inside, then there's no reason for anything to be used like lights, water or the T.V being turned on. This will greatly reduce the amount of energy you're using, which will also lower your utility bill. And as if that's not enough, being outside and doing something physical is also great for your health. If you are close enough to where you want to go, you could also bike or walk to save on transportation. During the warmer months, you could bike or walk to work and save tons!

Chapter 6: Reconciling Your Bank Statements

Reconciling your bank statements means to compare the bank's records to your own and check that they match. The purpose of this is to find any differences between the two. If there are any differences, then you'll have to change your records to match that of the bank or inform the bank of any errors they have made. In short, the point is to make sure your bank account's balance is correct. You should keep a record of all your deposits and spending so that you will be able to later match it up to your bank's records.

A big reason you should do this is to avoid fraud. Many people who commit fraud will first "test out" someone's bank account by making a few small purchases, and waiting to see if they notice the money has gone missing. If they do not, then they will go on to make bigger purchases. Many people may not check their bank accounts frequently enough, or pay close enough attention to be able to catch fraudulent activity on their account until it's already too late. By paying closer attention to your bank statements, especially those that do not match your records, you can catch and stop fraudulent activity faster, and prevent them from using your money for bigger purchases if you stop it quickly enough.

Another reason you should keep a record of your bank statements is to track fees. Some banks may start you out without a monthly service fee and add one later on. Others might require you to have a certain amount of money in your account to avoid getting a fee. Knowing this information could help you prevent getting unnecessary fees. It can also help you identify if you were incorrectly given a fee such as an incorrect overdraft fee. If you catch these things soon enough, then the bank can recognize them and see that it was a mistake. The longer you wait will make it harder on the bank to figure out if it should be there or not. If you wait too long on certain fees, you might even miss your opportunity to get it removed.

With the number of transactions banks do every single day, it's entirely possible for a mistake to happen. Keeping track of your spending and your bank account will help you spot any of these errors that may occur. It might even help you find errors in your records. Human error can happen, so when you pay close attention to the bank's records along with your own, it will prevent errors on both sides.

Online banking helps cut a lot of this workout, but you should still keep your own records of your spending and your deposits to make sure everything is correct. This is mostly helpful to businesses because they have a lot more spending to keep track of, than an individual person, and it's very important to track all of their spendings so that they can stay on budget.

Chapter 7: Plan for Retirement

You are never too young to start saving for retirement! The younger you start saving, the better as this will give the interest more chance to build the younger you start. There are many ways to save for retirement.

- 401(k) or 403(b)
    - o These will be offered by your employer and are probably the most common way to save for retirement. The money is withheld from your payroll and distributed directly into your account. This option is great because you aren't responsible for putting the money away yourself. It's taken out of your check every month automatically and you never see the money.

- Solo 401(k)
    - o This is the same concept as the previous saving options, only that you will do this individually and you are responsible for setting this account up.

- SEP IRA
    - o SEP stands for simplified employee pension and these are accounts that are easier to set up than a solo 401(k). This is typically used by anyone who is self-employed or a small business owner. If the business has any employees, then the employer to those who meet certain requirements.

- Simple IRA
  - This would also be an option for a small business owner. If you have less than 100 employees, this allows you to set up IRA's with less paperwork.

- IRA
  - You can contribute up to $5,500 a year to an IRA, and $6,500 if you're over 50 and this money grows tax-free. Anyone can use these accounts and you can also contribute to an IRA and 401(k) at the same time. But you cannot deduct your IRA contributions from your taxable income if you earn more than $71,000 annually.

- Roth IRA
  - With this option, you are contributing after-tax dollars. You get no tax deduction for your contribution. There is no mandatory withdrawal at age 70, and you can withdraw your contributions at any time without penalty.

Most people aim to retire at the age of 60. Using the rule of 25, you'll have to figure out how much money you spend or plan to spend annually and multiply that number by 25. So, if you need $40,000 every year, $40,000 x 25 = $1,000,000. That's how much you'll need in your retirement savings account by the time you are 60. Using this, you can get an idea of how much you'll need to have by the time you retire, and then you can take that number to figure out how much money you should put back for retirement every month to get to your desired goal.

When calculating what you should be saving for retirement, you should focus on spending, not necessarily your income. Your income can change many times throughout your life. If you start saving when you're 20, it's very possible you aren't going to have that same job or income when you're about to retire. In your early 20's, your income probably reflects an entry-level salary. It's likely you're going to have a few career changes or career advancements by the time you reach retirement age. The rule of thumb that your retirement should replace your income isn't entirely accurate. This is assuming that you are spending most of or all your income. Therefore, you should plan to have enough money for what you plan to spend, not to replace your current income. This can help if you're having problems finding the money in your budget to put into savings. You more than likely aren't spending your entire income so the amount you'll have to put back would not be as much.

Just like making a budget, planning for your retirement needs to suit your wants and needs. You may want to travel and live more extravagantly than before and need to be a heavy saver. Or maybe you plan on being a light spender who wants to live modestly in their retirement. Deciding the kind of life you want to live when you retire will be a factor when you are calculating how much you should save.

So, why is saving for your retirement so important? A retirement plan gives you a clear path to follow to be successful. You are essentially making a budget for yourself for the future. Once you reach a certain age, you may not want to or not be able to work anymore. You'll need enough money to be able to support yourself in your old age. You don't want to try to save too much and not be able to handle your budget, but you also don't want to chance running out of savings one day either.

There are a few steps to getting the most out of your retirement plan. You should start saving for retirement once you are debt free and have 3-6 months of living expenses saved. First, you should invest 15% of your gross income into a retirement plan that is tax-advantaged such as a 401(k) and a Roth IRA. Your goal here is to consistently save and keep on saving while you move onto other financial goals. The next step is to calculate what your retirement savings will be. You may even consider getting an investment advisor to help you with this. You should expect to be able to live off your retirement savings and not run out. If you do decide to use an investment advisor, they can help you to make sure you'll have enough money in your retirement plan to live off of, accounting for inflation at your expected retirement age and considering any taxes or fees that may later apply. The last step is to compare what you expect to have in savings compared to your monthly or yearly expenses now. You'll need enough money to pay for all of your expenses after calculating any extra costs you may have.

Just like your budget, what you want to get from your retirement will entirely depend upon your wants and your needs. What do you picture when you think about retirement? Is it at home with your spouse with a houseful of grandkids? Is it sitting by the beach on some tropical island? Do you want to stay in your home or sell it? What will you do all day? Will you continue working? Have you considered any medical care you may need? If you're young, it may be hard to answer these questions. It can be hard to think about life after retirement. There may be questions you didn't even think to ask yourself until after you've retired because you've never lived like that before. You don't know what it's like to not have to go to work, or to have this much free time. You'll need something to do to fill up all the extra time you'll have. If you aren't' sure what you want yet, you can start by saving the 15% like the first step mentioned. As you get older and begin to develop an idea of what you want your retirement to look like, you can change your savings plan accordingly.

Conclusion

In conclusion, we've learned how to make a budget and how to stick to it, how to make room for extra spending when we didn't previously have it, how to get out of the cycle of living paycheck-to-paycheck, why you should save before spending, how to get rid of unnecessary spending and how it can add up quickly if you aren't careful, how to save while creating less waste, why you should reconcile your bank statements, and how to create a retirement plan. I hope you are able to use this advice to create your own unique budget that works for you and start saving. You can use these tools to make your first budget, manage or change the budget you already have, learn new ways to make more money available to you, or help you to save more. And remember, it's never too late to make a budget or to start saving!

Phil C. Senior

www.ingramcontent.com/pod-product-compliance
Lightning Source LLC
Chambersburg PA
CBHW030537220526
45463CB00007B/2879